SHAWN MENDES

SINGER & SONGWRITER

DENNIS ST. SAUVER

Big Buddy Books

An Imprint of Abdo Publishing
abdobooks.com

BIG BUDDY POP BIOGRAPHIES

abdobooks.com

Published by Abdo Publishing, a division of ABDO, PO Box 398166, Minneapolis, Minnesota 55439.
Copyright © 2019 by Abdo Consulting Group, Inc. International copyrights reserved in all countries.
No part of this book may be reproduced in any form without written permission from the publisher.
Big Buddy Books™ is a trademark and logo of Abdo Publishing.

Printed in the United States of America, North Mankato, Minnesota.
102018
012019

Cover Photo: Frazer Harrison/Getty Images.
Interior Photos: Ben Gabbe/Getty Images (p. 11); Brad Barket/Getty Images (p. 19); Chris Young/
    AP Images (p. 17); Cooper Neill/Getty Images (p. 15); Dimitrios Kambouris/Getty Images (p. 29);
    Handout/Getty Images (p. 21); Kevin Winter/Getty Images (pp. 9, 23, 25); Larry Busacca/Getty
    Images (p. 13); Mark Blinch/AP Images (p. 5); Mike Coppola/Getty Images (p. 27).

Coordinating Series Editor: Tamara L. Britton
Contributing Series Editor: Jill M. Roesler
Graphic Design: Jenny Christensen, Cody Laberda

Library of Congress Control Number: 2018948440

Publisher's Cataloging-in-Publication Data

Names: St. Sauver, Dennis, author.
Title: Shawn Mendes / by Dennis St. Sauver.
Description: Minneapolis, Minnesota : Abdo Publishing, 2019 | Series: Big buddy
    pop biographies set 4 | Includes online resources and index.
Identifiers: ISBN 9781532118012 (lib. bdg.) | ISBN 9781532171055 (ebook)
Subjects: LCSH: Mendes, Shawn, 1998- --Juvenile literature. | Singers--
    Biography--Juvenile literature. | Popular music--Juvenile literature.
Classification: DDC 782.42164092 [B]--dc23

CONTENTS

AMAZING SINGER.................................. 4

SNAPSHOT 5

FAMILY TIES 6

EARLY YEARS....................................... 8

RISING STAR 10

SUPERSTAR..14

SONGWRITER 18

PERFORMANCES 22

AWARDS 24

GIVING BACK 26

BUZZ..28

GLOSSARY...30

ONLINE RESOURCES.............................31

INDEX 32

AMAZING SINGER

Shawn Mendes is a talented singer and songwriter. He started out by posting short videos of himself singing on the Internet. Within months, Shawn had a huge following of fans on **social media**!

DID YOU KNOW ?
Shawn taught himself to play the guitar by watching YouTube videos.

SNAPSHOT

NAME:
Shawn Peter Raul Mendes

BIRTHDAY:
August 8, 1998

BIRTHPLACE:
Toronto, Ontario, Canada

POPULAR ALBUMS:
*Handwritten, Illuminate,
Shawn Mendes*

FAMILY TIES

Shawn was born on August 8, 1998, in Toronto, Ontario, Canada. He is the son of Karen and Manuel Mendes. Karen is from England and Manuel is from Portugal.

Shawn has a younger sister, Aaliyah. She is very popular on **social media**.

DID YOU KNOW?

Shawn enjoys playing sports. He played soccer and ice hockey while in school.

WHERE IN THE WORLD?

CANADA

Quebec

Ontario

LAKE HURON

Toronto

LAKE ONTARIO

Michigan

New York

LAKE ERIE

UNITED STATES

Ohio

Pennsylvania

ATLANTIC OCEAN

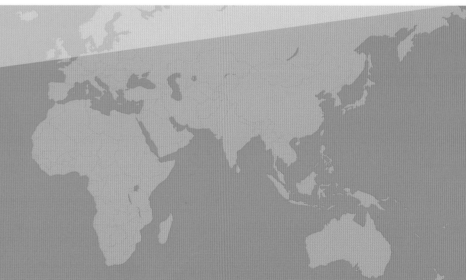

N
W   E
S

EARLY YEARS

Shawn began posting videos of himself singing in 2013. One year later, he signed a record deal with Island Records.

He had to leave high school during his junior year to go on tour. But Shawn kept up with his classes online. In June 2016, he **graduated** with the rest of his class.

DID YOU KNOW ?
Before he became a singer, Shawn wanted to be an actor.

Shawn was just 13 when he started to play the guitar.

RISING STAR

Shawn **released** his first single "Life of the Party" in June 2014. In only 37 minutes, it hit number one on the iTunes Top Albums chart!

Later that year, he came out with *The Shawn Mendes **EP***. It soared to number five on the *Billboard* 200 chart. Shawn was on his way to becoming a superstar.

The Shawn Mendes EP sold nearly 50,000 copies in its first week.

In 2015, Shawn **released** his first full-length album called *Handwritten*. It immediately jumped to number one on the *Billboard* Top Albums chart.

All of the songs on the album were very popular. But the song "Stitches" was a major hit. It was on the *Billboard* Hot 100 chart for 52 weeks!

DID YOU KNOW ?
Shawn held his first-ever concert on November 10, 2013. He was just 15 years old.

Shawn was the opening act for Taylor Swift during her 1989 tour in 2014.

SUPERSTAR

In 2016, the superstar put out his second album called *Illuminate*. The album showed how much Shawn's talent had grown in just one year.

That December, he **released** a special album called *Live at Madison Square Garden*. It featured live songs from a concert he **performed** earlier that year.

Shawn sang with Camila Cabello in the song "I Know What You Did Last Summer." It reached number 20 on *Billboard's* Hot 100 chart.

While working hard on his music, Shawn met one of his **role models**, John Mayer. The two **performed** a song together during one of John's concerts in 2017.

In April 2017, Shawn went on a world tour to **promote** the *Illuminate* album. He played 60 concerts for fans across the world.

DID YOU KNOW

Shawn was an opening act for singer Austin Mahone in 2014.

Shawn won the Allan Slaight Award in 2015. It honors young stars that make a positive impact in music, film, or the arts.

SONGWRITER

Shawn is a very talented singer and guitar player. But he is also good at writing his own songs. The **lyrics** often tell a personal story about his life.

The singer does not write all of his songs. But even if he does not write it, he is still a major part of the process.

In 2016, Shawn was a lead singer at Radio City Music Hall in New York City, New York.

Shawn has won three BMI **Awards** for songwriters. His songs "Treat You Better," "Mercy," and "There's Nothing Holdin' Me Back" all won awards for his talented writing.

Not only does Shawn enjoy writing, but he also likes to read. He is a big fan of Harry Potter. He visited The Wizarding World of Harry Potter in Orlando, Florida in 2015.

PERFORMANCES

Fans have loved to see Shawn **perform** since his **career** first began. In 2016, he was the musical guest on *Saturday Night Live*.

In 2017, Shawn sang his hit song "There's Nothing Holdin' Me Back" at the MTV Music **Awards**. Three months later, he performed the same song at the American Music Awards in Los Angeles, California.

Shawn sang "In My Blood" at the *Billboard* Music Awards in May 2018.

AWARDS

Shawn has amazing talent. He has been **nominated** for more than 120 **awards**!

He won a Kids' Choice Award for Favorite New Artist in 2016. Then he won the same award for Favorite Male Singer in 2017 and 2018.

In 2014 and 2015, he won the Teen Choice Award for Most Popular Web Star for music. And in 2016, he earned Best **International** Artist from BBC Radio 1 Teen Awards.

The young artist has won more than 40 awards for singing or songwriting.

TEEN CHOICE

GIVING BACK

Shawn loves to give back to important causes. He has supported Musicians On Call. This **organization** uses music to help sick **patients** and their families.

In 2014, Shawn and DoSomething.org started a campaign called "Notes from Shawn." The movement addressed sadness and low **self-esteem**.

Shawn always makes an effort to connect with his fans. He often takes photos with them.

BUZZ

Shawn has kept very busy over the past five years. And no matter what he does, he always seems to rise to the top. Fans are excited to see what Shawn does next!

DID YOU KNOW ?

Shawn Mendes: The Tour begins in March 2019. He will tour through Europe and North America promoting the *Shawn Mendes* album.

In 2018, Shawn was included in *Time* magazine's list of the 100 Most Influential People.

GLOSSARY

award something that is given in recognition of good work or a good act.

career a period of time spent in a certain job.

EP extended play. A music recording with more than one song, but fewer than a full album.

graduate (GRA-juh-wayt) to complete a level of schooling.

international (in-tuhr-NASH-nuhl) of or relating to more than one nation.

lyrics the words to a song.

nominate to name as a possible winner.

organization (ohr-guh-nuh-ZAY-shuhn) a group of people united for a common purpose.

patient (PAY-shehnt) a person who is under the care of a doctor.

perform to do something in front of an audience. A performance is the act of doing something, such as singing or acting, in front of an audience.

promote to help something become known.

release to make available to the public.

role model a person who other people respect and try to act like.

self-esteem (self-UH-steem) a feeling of satisfaction that someone has in himself or herself and his or her own abilities.

social media a form of communication on the Internet where people can share information, messages, and videos. It may include blogs and online groups.

Booklinks
NONFICTION NETWORK
FREE! ONLINE NONFICTION RESOURCES

To learn more about Shawn Mendes, visit **abdobooklinks.com**. These links are routinely monitored and updated to provide the most current information available.

INDEX

award shows **22, 23**

awards **17, 20, 24, 25**

Cabello, Camila **15**

California **22**

Canada **5, 6**

charities **26**

England **6**

Europe **28**

family **6**

Florida **21**

Handwritten (album) **5, 12**

Harry Potter **21**

hobbies **6, 21**

Illuminate (album) **5, 14, 16**

Island Records **8**

Live at Madison Square Garden (album) **14**

Mahone, Austin **16**

Mayer, John **16**

music charts **10, 12, 13, 15**

music tours **8, 12, 16, 28**

New York **19**

North America **28**

Portugal **6**

Radio City Music Hall **19**

Saturday Night Live (television show) **22**

Shawn Mendes (album) **5, 28**

Shawn Mendes EP, The (EP) **10, 11**

social media **4, 6, 8**

Swift, Taylor **13**

Time (magazine) **29**

Wizarding World of Harry Potter, The **21**